11/16   - 3

Learning About Earning

Rachel Eagen

 Crabtree Publishing Company

www.crabtreebooks.com

Money $ense
An Introduction to Financial Literacy

Author: Rachel Eagen

Series research and development: Reagan Miller

Editors: Reagan Miller and Janine Deschenes

Designer: Tammy McGarr

Photo research: Tammy McGarr and Crystal Sikkens

Proofreader: Crystal Sikkens

Prepress technician: Tammy McGarr

Print and production coordinator: Katherine Berti

Photographs

Thinkstock: monkeybusinessimages: p 7 (top left);
    kzenon: p 7 (middle right); David Sacks: p 14

Shutterstock: © Rob Wilson: p 17 (middle right);

All other images from Shutterstock

Library and Archives Canada Cataloguing in Publication

Eagen, Rachel, 1979-, author
    Learning about earning / Rachel Eagen.

(Money sense : an introduction to financial literacy)
Includes index.
Issued in print and electronic formats.
ISBN 978-0-7787-2665-4 (hardback).--
ISBN 978-0-7787-2669-2 (paperback).--
ISBN 978-1-4271-1801-1 (html)

    1. Finance, Personal--Juvenile literature. 2. Income--Juvenile
literature. 3. Wages--Juvenile literature. I. Title.

HG179.E2 2016   j332.024   C2016-904169-7
                                           C2016-904170-0

Library of Congress Cataloging-in-Publication Data

Names: Eagen, Rachel, 1979-, author.
Title: Learning about earning / Rachel Eagen.
Description: New York : Crabtree Publishing Company, [2017] |
    Series: Money sense : an introduction to financial literacy | Includes index.
Identifiers: LCCN 2016026956 (print) | LCCN 2016036644 (ebook) |
    ISBN 9780778726654 (reinforced library binding) |
    ISBN 9780778726692 (pbk.) |
    ISBN 9781427118011 (Electronic HTML)
Subjects: LCSH: Wages--Juvenile literature. | Labor--Juvenile literature. |
    Finance--Juvenile literature.
Classification: LCC HD4909 .E24 2017 (print) | LCC HD4909 (ebook) |
    DDC 331.2/1--dc23
LC record available at https://lccn.loc.gov/2016026956

Crabtree Publishing Company

www.crabtreebooks.com   1-800-387-7650

Printed in Canada/082016/TL20160715

Published in Canada
Crabtree Publishing
616 Welland Ave.
St. Catharines, Ontario
L2M 5V6

Published in the United States
Crabtree Publishing
PMB 59051
350 Fifth Avenue, 59th Floor
New York, New York 10118

Published in the United Kingdom
Crabtree Publishing
Maritime House
Basin Road North, Hove
BN41 1WR

Published in Australia
Crabtree Publishing
3 Charles Street
Coburg North
VIC 3058

Table of Contents

Why do People Need Money?

People need money to buy **goods** and **services** that meet their needs and wants. Some goods and services are needs and other goods and services are wants.

A family trip to an amusement park is a want.

4

Needs and wants

A need is something we must have to **survive**. Examples of needs are food, shelter, and clothing. A want is something we would like to have. Examples of wants are junk food, toys, and movie tickets.

Make "cents" of it!

Read the list below. Decide whether each item is a need or a want.

- A jacket for cold weather
- A television
- A trip to the zoo

How do People Earn Money?

People earn money by working. When people work, they are paid money for their time and skills.

The money people earn is called an **income**.

There are many different types of **jobs** in the world. People use their skills, education, or interests to do their jobs.

Why do people work?

People use money to pay for things they need and want. Parents work to earn an income so that they can pay for the wants and needs of their families as well as themselves.

Getting Paid

People can earn their income in different ways. Some people work in jobs where they are paid a certain amount for each hour of work. This is called a **wage**. They may work different hours each day, for different numbers of days per week.

These people are earning a wage by working in a supermarket.

Some people may earn an income by starting their own **business**. A business provides goods or services that people need or want.

Poppy's Bakery

Ways to earn

Other people work the same amount of hours every day, for the same number of days each week. They get paid the same amount of money each year for their work. This is called a **salary**.

Goods and Services

Some people earn money by growing or making goods to sell. Goods are objects we can touch and hold, such as food or clothing. Bakers make food for people to eat. They earn money by selling goods.

Toys are goods we buy.

Working for others

Some people earn money by providing services to others. Services are work that people do for other people. For example, swimming instructors earn money by teaching people how to swim.

Swimming lessons and taking the bus are services we pay for.

Make "**cents**" of it!

Read the list of jobs below. Which people provide services, and which people make and sell goods?

- **A car** mechanic, **or someone who fixes cars**
- **A potato farmer**
- **A dentist**

Producers and Consumers

The people who make goods or provide services are called **producers**. The people who buy goods or pay for services are called **consumers**.

This farmer is a producer of tomatoes.

This woman is a consumer of tomatoes.

Earning and spending

People can be both producers and consumers. To earn money, a person has to be a producer, or make goods or provide services. To get the things they need, a person also has to be a consumer, or buy goods and services.

Make "cents" of it!

Read the sentences below. For each, decide whether Ramon is a producer or a consumer.

- Ramon makes and sells lemonade in front of his house.
- Ramon pays for tennis lessons.
- Ramon buys a birthday present for his friend.

The Economic System

When people make goods or provide services, and then sell them to consumers for money, and then spend that money on their own goods and services, they are part of an economic system.

Anyone can be part of an economic system when they buy or sell goods and services.

A small farmers' market brings together producers and consumers in a community.

A system that works

An economic system is made up of all the producers and consumers in an area. A system can include an area as small as your community or as large as the whole world. The system needs people to buy and sell goods and services to work. Everyone has a part.

Spend or Save?

Most people do not spend all of the money that they earn right away. They **save** money for things that they might need in the future. People also save money for **unexpected** things, such as fixing a car if it breaks down.

When household items such as washing machines break down, parents have to spend money to fix or replace them. This is an unexpected expense.

Long-term saving

Some goods and services
cost a lot of money,
such as cars, houses,
or college **tuition**. People
need to save part of their
income over a long period
of time to buy these
goods and services.

Kids can Earn!

Many kids earn a weekly allowance, or an amount of money given to them every week by their parents. Usually, they have to help their families with household chores to earn their allowance.

Many kids receive money as a gift from friends or relatives on their birthday.

18

Kids can earn money by providing services to the people around them.

Fun ways to earn

Some kids earn money in other ways. They might provide services, such as shoveling a neighbor's driveway in the winter, or raking leaves off of their lawn in the fall. They might sell goods, such as in a bake sale or at a lemonade stand.

Your Turn to Earn

There are a lot of ways to learn about earning. How will you earn money one day? Ask your parents about spending and saving for your family's wants and needs.

Ask your parents about their first jobs. What kind of work did they do? What did they do with the money they earned?

Part of the system

The economic system needs producers and consumers to make, provide, sell, and buy goods and services. What wants and needs do you have? Think of ways you can be a producer and earn money. Then, you can be a consumer, and buy the things you need or want.

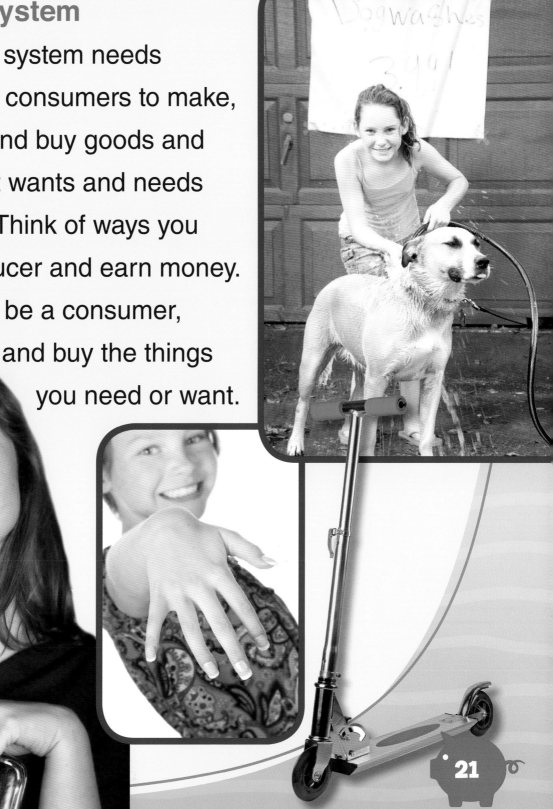

Learning More

Books

First, Rachel. *What's It Worth: Fun with Coins & Bills*.
Minnesota: Abdo Publishing. 2016.

Rosinksy, Natalie M. *All About Money*.
Minneapolis: Compass Point Books. 2004.

Rosinksy, Natalie M. *Earning Money*.
Minneapolis: Compass Point Books. 2004.

Vermond, Kira. *The Secret Life of Money: A Kid's Guide to Cash*.
Toronto: Owlkids Books Inc. 2011.

Websites

Rich Kid Smart Kid
www.richkidsmartkid.com

The United States Mint: H.I.P. Pocket Change
www.usmint.gov/kids

Sense and Dollars
senseanddollars.thinkport.org

How to Make Money as a Kid
www.howtomakemoneyasakid.com/ways-to-make-money-as-a-kid

Words to Know

business (BIZ-nis) noun Selling goods or services in the hope of making money

consumer (kuh n-SOO-mer) noun A person that buys goods or pays for services

goods (goo ds) noun Items that you can touch and hold

income (IN-kuhm) noun Money received for providing goods or services

job (job) noun A task done for a set amount of money

mechanic (muh-kan-ik) noun A person who fixes machinery, tools, or equipment

producer (pruh-DOO-ser) noun A person who makes goods or provides a service

salary (SAL-uh-ree) noun A certain amount of money, based on the same hours worked throughout the year, that is paid at set times

save (seyv) verb To keep or avoid spending

services (SUR-vises) noun Work done for others to make money

survive (ser-VAHYV) verb To stay alive

tuition (too-ISH-uh n) noun The amount of money charged by a school for teaching

unexpected (uhn-ik-SPEK-tid) adjective Surprising or not expected

wage (weyj) noun A certain amount of money paid for each hour of work

A noun is a person, place, or thing.

A verb is an action word that tells you what someone or something does.

An adjective is a word that tells you what something is like.

23

Index

About the Author

Rachel Eagen studied Creative Writing and English Literature at university. Now, she edits and writes books for a living. She is the author of 18 other books for children and youth. When she was 11, she spent her summer selling pop at a golf course. She used her earnings to buy her first mountain bike.